THE NO MATTER WHAT CLUB 90 NUGGETS FOR THE FIRST 90 DAYS OF RECOVERY

THE ROAD TO SUCCESS – A Life Long Journey

NOTE FROM THE AUTHOR

First of all, giving God all the glory and the honor for blessing me with a new way of life and another day clean. God has truly blessed me and He has blessed me to be a blessing to others. I do not take my gift for granted, neither do I take my transformed life for granted. If it had not been for God's love and his grace and mercy I would not be able to provide you with this blessing of hope and encouragement for your road to a clean and successful life in recovery. This book is a composite of nuggets from my recovery experiences that fostered my mindset of the importance of accepting that NO MATTER WHAT as a two- fold message. First, I believe that God will take care of me, take me through, make a way, and provide my needs NO MATTER WHAT. Second, I believe that I cannot get high or drunk NO MATTER WHAT because I cannot control it and it will not solve any of my problems.

Thanks to all of those prayer warriors that prayed me through, my anointed and praying grandmother, Flora Spearman, who was faithful to God for my transformation and to Kennett Pilgrim, who showed me the way to a new way of life, and my faithful and devoted husband, Dexter Anderson, who is my greatest fan and cheerleader. And to my children, Dexter Jr., Tamika, Marquetta, and Heather, thanks for allowing me to be your motivator and mother.

Thanks to my Pastor, Delwynn Williams, who preached me through my darkest days and to the members of the Joyous St. John Missionary Baptist Church for your support and prayers. Finally, to my Soror Johna Pittman for the cover design, my Soror Janice Lucas for the foreword, my friend Barbara Copeland for editing and illustrations, and ALL of my Recovery Family. My prayer is that those who are reading this book will gain hope and encouragement to not give up on the process and to build a stronger relationship with God.

Foreword

The Road to a Successful New Way of Life

Three months, 90 days, 2,160 hours, 129,600 minutes: The time it will take you to complete this recovery path toward becoming the person that you want to be can be measured in numbers, but the life-changing possibility is immeasurable. The hard work that you do through this meditative journey will be your path to becoming who you want to be. The author of this journey, Minister Dr. Tammy Anderson, has created this pathway from her experience. She embodies the kind of change that can happen in your life, too. Through trials and tribulations, she emerged a purpose driven spirit who escaped from darkness into the marvelous light. Dr. Anderson knows firsthand the inner work that is needed to make change happen in one's life. It takes daily work: reading, journaling, and meditating. Follow this journey with an open heart, open mind and belief in yourself. Write in this journal, especially when it hurts. Successful completion of this 90-day journey is a key factor to your long term recovery. Research studies have concluded that making it through the first 90 days without a relapse indicates a greater chance of staying free from the addiction that has held you hostage in the past. So, in this forward, I encourage you to move forward—one day at a time—to the new you who awaits.

Introduction

I have been clean for 22 and half years but I have been in recovery for 17 years. You do the math. I have learned the importance of recovery from a destructive fall in my life while clean and not in recovery. Because of the lesson that I learned I found it necessary to provide those who are coming into recovery with recovery nuggets to encourage and motivate them to stay in recovery and to be successful on this road to recovery.

One thing that I learned early in recovery while in treatment was that I could never get high again "NO Matter What!" I gleaned this revelation from watching the movie "Losing Isaiah" while I was in treatment. I accepted that I had to become a member of that group that I call today "The No Matter What Club." This club is for those who can admit and accept that they cannot successfully get high or drunk no matter what. By accepting membership into this club, you are declaring and decreeing that no matter what, getting high or drunk will not fix your problems and the only thing that it will change is your clean date or residence. In other words it will give you a new place to reside: jails, institutions, or death. Getting high or drunk for these members is no longer an option because we accept that it is not the solution to our problems, instead it will only make your life worse. When you are faced with struggles, dilemmas, trials and tribulations, No matter what this too shall pass. Trouble don't last always! I encourage you if you are accepting this new way of life in recovery that you also accept membership into this club.

I realized that admittance to having a problem is easy but accepting that I can no longer use again has been the issue for many who start this way of life. Instead of focusing on what you are losing I recommend that you focus on what you are gaining … a happy, joyous, and free life. Think about ALL the benefits you gain when you are not using. Focus on all that is restored in your life when you are not using.

Congratulations on accepting this new way of life and membership into the greatest club of recovery... The No Matter What Club! You have made the best decision that you could ever make in your life! Welcome to a greater life, a happier life, a life with many opportunities, a life of peace and serenity, a LIFE! You are no longer just existing you are now living. May God bless your life as you travel this road called Recovery!

Day 1
I cannot successfully get high or drunk period!
(Dr. Tammy)

After accepting that I am an addict the next step is to accept the fact based on my past attempts and tries to control my using with no avail, that I cannot control my high or drunk successfully. I am powerless over my using once I start using. If I tell myself this when the urge, cravings, or thoughts enter my mind, I am one step closer to a successful journey in recovery. I remember thinking the first time that I went to treatment that I could control my using and that I could get high with finesse. Well my disease lied to me once more telling me I could control it better this time and that I could handle my using in moderation without it taking control over my life. It worked for a little while, so that it could fool me but eventually I was right back to where I started, in bondage to the disease.

Recovery Insight: When I start using I am never successful in how I use…..No matter what!

Day 2
You are right where you're supposed to be! #Kennett Pilgrim

Acceptance in life is learning to recognize that wherever you are in your life is part of the assignment to fulfilling your purpose in your life. I always had the tendency to focus so much on the fact I was not where my former plans in my life had charted me to be at that point in my life, so I found myself tripping over my failures and my defeats. My sponsor would always remind me that where I was today is right where I was supposed to be. This was a huge state of acceptance for me! I learned that "It is what it is and it ain't what it ain't."

Recovery Insight: Accept your present as a part of your future…. No matter what!

Day 3
Insanity is repeating the same behavior expecting different results. #Anonymous

You cannot expect things in your life to change for the better until you learn to do something different from what you were doing. My results in my life are based on what I'm doing repeatedly in my life. Nothing changes if nothing changes, if you always do what you've always done, you will always get what you've always got. If you want something different you must do something different. It is insane to think that this time I will use different so therefore, it will be different. Yes it will be different, it will be worse!

Recovery Insight: It is insane to look for a different result from the same actions… No matter what!

Day 4
Feelings are not a fact it's just a fact that you are feeling.
#Anonymous

Facts are things which remain the same no matter what. Feelings never stay the same, they change based on time, experiences, or situations. But they do change! One minute you can feel angry, frustrated, disgusted, disappointed, heartbroken, broken hearted, rejected, abandoned, hungry, lonely, and tired; however, these emotions can change with a talk with your sponsor, sharing in a meeting, journaling, prayer, rest, food, or reading inspirational books. There is a solution for whatever you are feeling if you seek the solution instead of staying in the problem.

Recovery Insight: I have the power to change my feelings if I choose… No matter what!

Day 5

You can plan a plan but you cannot plan a result. You must have a plan or you will become a part of someone else's plan. #Dr. Tammy

In life you must have a plan of direction or destination. This plan gives you purpose and meaning in your life. You cannot base your entire life on the results of one plan because they are not guaranteed. It is important to have a plan because you will have a sense of direction and a course of life to follow otherwise you will end up following others and lose all sense of your life's purpose. When seeking my life's purpose it was essential that I took an inventory of my life experiences. These experiences created my passion and inevitably shaped my purpose. I have learned that life's purpose is birthed out of life challenges and changes.

Recovery Insight: Planning is essential but praying for purpose is priority… No matter what!

Day 6
Don't let fear block your blessings! FEAR is simply False Evidence Appearing Real #Anonymous

Fear is an emotion that can stop us from continuing on our journey in life. It can cause us to miss out on our blessings because it can paralyze us and prevent us from moving forward in our journey of recovery. I found it to be extremely important that I learned to listen to those who had quality clean time as opposed to my own thoughts. I had to be reminded that it was my own thoughts that got me in the shape that I was in. In my first months of recovery I had so many doubts of being able to stay clean and thoughts of never being able to amount to anything that was meaningful or productive. Becoming a productive member of society had become a figment of my imagination. It was people in recovery who encouraged me and talked me through my fears to a place and mindset of hope.

Recovery Insight: I'm learning to Face Everything and Recover... No matter what!

Day 7
You must go to the same length that you went to for your high also for your recovery #Anonymous

Whatever length you went to for drugs and alcohol, you must use that same tenacity in your journey of recovery. When things seem too difficult or somewhat impossible; press with all you have with the attitude "No matter what I've got to have it." I realized when I first got into recovery that I could not whine and complain what I did not have, all the suggestions that I was given, all the meetings that I needed to attend (90 meetings in 90 days), and how I was going to spend time with my family, work and do recovery. I accepted after I was given this nugget that I had to let nothing come before my recovery and I had to go for it as though it was a matter of life and death.

Recovery Insight: Same push, same press…No matter what!

Day 8
Behind anger are hurt, fear, and frustration.
 # Dr. Tammy

There is more to an emotion besides anger. Typically a person uses anger to deal with their hurtful feelings. When a person has been hurt, to prevent further hurt they will build a wall to prevent others from getting close to them called anger. Anger is also a defensive mechanism used to deal with fear. When I am fearful of the results or the outcome I use anger to cover my fear. I have also recognized that anger is another way of responding to my frustration. Instead of operating in anger I had to learn to identify my real feelings and share them instead of my anger.

Recovery Insight: I must learn to identify my real feelings…No matter what!

Day 9
On my bad days I seek you, on my good days I thank you, on my great days I praise you, but every day I need you thank you God for always being here for me. #Anonymous

If I seek God every day in every situation I will always be in his presences and no matter what I am going through. When I reflect on the unmanageability that was in my life during my time of using I am able to see the handiwork of a power greater than myself working on my behalf, protecting me from hurt and danger and yet providing for me in my time of distraught and drought. No matter how I have felt about God and questioned the presence and the provisions of God it is apparent he was always there to love me and to carry me through the darkness within my life. Early in my recovery I built a closer relationship with God based on the recollection of the times that I reflected on my past and realized that He looked beyond my faults and saw my needs and blessed me in spite of me.

Recovery Insight: God can and God will if I let him… No matter what!

Day 10
When you choose to forgive you choose to be free. #Dr. Tammy

I cannot be liberated from my past until I deal with it and let it go. As long as I run from my past it will run after me. Secrets will make me sick and will eventually kill me. I take the power from my past when I share it with someone that I trust. I will always be in bondage to my past and my pain if I do not face it and slay it. I must learn to forgive those who have harmed me if want to be set free. I had to learn that as long as I held vengeance and victim in my heart I will always be controlled by those emotions. But if I learn to face those feelings head on and accept the fact that something in my life I am not responsible for and some things in my life I am responsible for yet all things in my life I can find forgiveness for. Once I learned to forgive those who hurt me including myself I was able to heal and be liberated from my past and my pain.

Recovery Insight: I must learn to forgive to move forward....No matter what!

Day 11
There is no passion to be found playing small – in settling for a life that is less than the one you are capable of living
#Pastor Anthony Andrews

I can operate in fear and fail to take the risks in my life or I can operate in faith and take the risk to fail and take a chance on my dreams in life. My disease will make me think that I can do things that I cannot do and tell me that I cannot do things that I can do. It is up to me to take the risk to go out in the deep and take a chance on something that I have never tried, the suggestions of recovery, and live that has proven to be a life that is happy, joyous, and free. I had to make a decision early in recovery to either continue on the path of destruction or to try a new way of life and get the life I deserved.

**Recovery Insight: I can no longer settle for less than I deserve..
No matter what!**

Day 12
God will take what's precious to you to get to you. #Dr. Tammy

Sometimes in order to get our attention god will take away or affect something is precious to you to get your attention. When God does this it is not to punish you but to prepare you for the purpose that he has promised you in your life. When we are so lost in our self-will running riot God will take what we treasure the most to get our attention to redirect us on our path; especially when we have drifted so far from him. It is difficult to accept what is best from us when we feel that we are losing something that is so important to us. I have learned that sometimes I have had to lose to win and some things had to be removed because they were not for my good, while others had to be repositioned for my betterment.

Recovery Insight: Sometimes we have to lose our treasure in order to find our gold mine ..No matter what!

Day 13
Get real…let's heal!   #Dr. B Caldwell

Until you get honest and real about the severity of your issue you cannot get better. I have to break down and get real about my situation before I can even recognize that I have a problem, a sickness, a dilemma. I cannot heal if I do not take care of my illness! Getting real means getting honest with myself! When I first started this journey of recovery, the first thing that I was told was not to pick up that first one and to become self-honest.

Recovery Insight: Until you admit your worse to will never get to your better.. No matter what

Day 14
Grudges are the heaviest weight to carry. Let your pain produce a purpose.

If I continue to hold on to my past pains and hurts and allow them to control me I will only produce more problems for myself. But when I seal with my past pains and hurts I can allow them to become the catalyst of my victory. In other words when I will turn my stumbling blocks into my stepping stones, I can step out of my mess into my bless by using my test as my testimony and my mess as message to bless someone else. I had to learn to let go of my grudges through prayer and working a 12 Step program. Once I was able to learn to forgive I then learned to use my experiences as a blessing to others who are struggling with the same situations that I have found my healing.

Recovery Insight: Turn your pain into passion and your passion into your purpose.. No matter what!

Day 15
When I lost all my excuses I found my results
#Dr. Tammy

When there are no more rationalizations or justifications in my thoughts and mouth I am forced to reckon with the reality of my life and that is where my life awaits. I can now start living and stop just existing. The solutions to my problems appear when I no longer lived in my excuses. My results are where my letting go of my past, pain, I can't, and they won't, will stop and my healing, I can, and the No matter what mindset will start.

Recovery Insight: I've got to surrender to losing myself in order to find myself .. No matter what!

Day 16
FAITH Is Forsaking ALL instead Trust Him #Pastor Delwynn G. Williams

In life you will have learn how to abandon thoughts of doubt and fear and replace them with trust in God. When you find yourself doubting whether or not you can take this new way of life or survive the expectations of this new way of life that is when you have to renounce and give up the temptations of what might have temporarily felt good for the sake of something that has a lifetime of being happy, joyous, and free. I had to learn to break up with my love affair with destruction so that I could build a relationship with God and have a life of true happiness.

Recovery Insight: Turning my back to destruction and walking a faith walk in a life of recovery will always take you to a happy place .. No matter what!

Day 17

God not only wants your whole heart … He wants your heart whole. #Dr. Tammy

God wants to heal you and make you whole again. He is not just interested in you giving your life to Him; He is interested in you surrendering your will and way to him as well. Surrendering implies that you are giving your control of the way you think, feel, and act over to Him so that He can transform your life into a new life that is happy, joyous and free. Do you want to be happy? Well, you can if you choose to let go and let God. When I go to the place of being "sick and tired of being sick and tired", that is when I gave up the ghost of believing that I can do this thing called live by myself. That is when I accepted that I needed help, that is when I accepted that I did not have the power to change by myself. I could not go just show up for surgery for a heart transplant and not allow the doctor to perform the surgery if I wanted to be healed, I had to consent to the surgery and trust the physician to heal me and make me whole. I encourage you to allow God to heal you and make your heart whole today.

Recovery Insight: I must prepare myself to give my ALL to receive what all that I need from God… No matter what!

Day 18
Life is 10% of what you make it and 90% of how you take it #Thomas W.

It is not what we do to make our life great instead it is how we deal with the things that happen within our lives that makes us great and successful. Dealing with life on life terms is a form of acceptance that gives us peace and serenity to handle whatever life throws us with self- control, fortitude, and dignity. I am powerless over people, places, and things. But I am not powerless over my actions and my behaviors. My perceptions of my situation have a lot to do with how I take and deal with what is happening in my life and around me.

Recovery Insight: How I take it determines how I make it through... No matter what!

Day 19
When I come into recovery I need to change…Everything!
#Anonymous

Changing people, places, and things is essential in making the necessary changes I need for my new way of life. I can no longer hang around the same people that I did when I was using, I cannot go to the same places that I did when I was using, and I cannot keep doing the same things that I did when I was using. The thinking that I used has to change, because my best thinking got me in the situation that I was in. Change is a process, especially when you are changing everything about yourself. This is a brand new way of life! It is not what you were before you started using it is who you will become when you deal with the issues that started you to using. I remember asking God to change me back to the person that I was before I started using without realizing that the drugs were just a symptom of my problem and not the core of my problem. I would only cycle back to the place of using if I did not accept my new way of life.

Recovery Insight: I have to change daily for the rest of my life… No matter what!

Day 20
It's better to be sitting in a meeting not wanting to be there than to be in active addiction wanting to be in a meeting.
#Anonymous

When you think that you want to complain about the suggestion of 90 meetings in 90 days, sometimes it is necessary to reflect on the times when you were in active addiction and feeling worthless, hopeless, shameful, broken and wanting a new way of life and didn't know where to start. It was so important that I did not forget the pain of using when I did not want to accept the suggestions of recovery and all the meetings. I had to be mindful of the fact that this was the greatest investment that I could make into my future of being happy, joyous. And free. We found ourselves crying and pleading for something more and now that we have more we want less. This disease is very tricky so I must be vigilant over my recovery and embrace the more of recovery.

Recovery Insight: Acceptance of more for my future will always require more of my commitment … No matter what!

Day 21

Being meek don't make you weak, it's means that you have total self control. #Thomas W.

Being meek is a manner of not allowing life to control you but, remaining calm in the storms, trials and tribulations within your life. When you are meek you are not being weak and allowing others to control your life instead being content and trusting God.

Recovery Insight: I don't always have to speak instead…No matter what!

Day 22

In every day there are 1,440 minutes. That means we have 1,440 daily opportunities to make a positive impact.
#Anonymous

I have 1,440 choices that I can Make in one day. I can choose to focus in my problems or I can focus on my blessings. When I focus more on others than myself I have less time to focus on my problems.

Recovery Insight: I have a choice to focus on my problems or focus on others… No matter what.!

Day 23
Recovery is like thanking your younger self for knowing how to push all the way through. #Dr. Tammy

Recovery allows you to pull of the layers that you have built around yourself in life these layers were created as a means of self practice and projection. Recovery provides steps that are tools to break the chains of bondage and the innocence of who you really are

Recovery Insight: Recovery heals the wounded inner child…No matter what!

Day 24

God Life is like a game of Tonk. You are dealt 5 cards. Within 2 to 3 pulls from the deck your entire game can change. However, like Tonk you could have the worst hand and win within 2 to three minutes. Good or bad hand it's not the hand it's how you play your hand. #Maya Sly

Life is like a game. You must learn the rule to the game and play the game with violating the rules. You can be creative and innovative but you must follow the rules. Life is 10 % of what you make it and 90% of how you take it. It is important that we always remember that nothing stays the same, everything will change. Acceptance the possibility of change is accepting the fact that we can plan a plan but we cannot plan a result. It is so important to learn to not give up before the game is over. Do not throw the towel in until the final second of the game. I have witnessed too many games won at the last seconds and minutes of the game. Our disease wants to kill us so it tells us that we can do things that we can't and that we can't do things that we can. The serenity prayer puts life in the proper perspective that we do not get it twisted but that we are able to center our thoughts around the fact that there is always hope. The solution is asking for the serenity to accept the things that I cannot change and the courage to change the things that I can and most of all the wisdom to know the difference. The winning move is seeking the wisdom to know the difference in what move to make.

Recovery Insight: Life is like a card game and realize it's not over until it's over…No matter what!

Day 25
The next step you take determines which door opens for you. #Dr. Tammy

The directions we take in our life determines the blessings that we experience. If we travel a road of destruction the door that opens for us will be destructive. If we travel the road of recovery the door that will open for us will be happy, joyous, and free.

Recovery Insight: You choose your destiny…No matter what!

Day 26
Mistakes are always forgivable if one has the courage to admit them. #Anonymous

It is easier to be forgiven with an apology than if one ignores their actions. It takes courage to admit when you are wrong. Courage brings correction, closure

Recovery Insight: Don't allow fear to cause you to miss your forgiveness…No matter what!

Day 27
Courage is being scared to death and saddling up anyway.

When life throws you situations that seem painful or downright impossible it is courage that overrides our fears and option of checking out to

Recovery Insight: Don't break down, break through…No matter what!

Day 28
Time decides who you meet in life, your heart decides who you want in your life, and your behavior decides who steps into your life.

Timing is everything! Because time is so important. It is important that you maximize your seconds, minutes and hours within a day. Being at the right place at the right time is crucial: My heart if hurt be guarded so that I don't allow anyone and everyone in my behavior is everything in deciding who wants to be a part of my life.

Recovery Insight: Time/ Heart/ Behavior…No matter what!

Day 29
Fortitude is strength of the mind. #Thomas W.

Fortitude is synonymous to courage, bravery, endurance, resilience, moral fiber, strength of character, strong mindedness and backbone. When life hits you and it will in either a great positive way or hard and painful way you must be equipped with the mental and emotional strength to face difficult adversities, danger, or temptation in a courageous manner.

Recovery Insight: Stay the course…No matter what!

Day 30
If I serve people I can miss God, but if I serve God I will not miss people.

Focusing on pleasing people and making your decisions in life based on wanting to satisfy and be accepted by people can cause a person to miss out on their God given purpose. However, if one serves God to please and satisfy Him then they will never miss neither God nor the people that they are purposed to serve. People pleasing was always a big problem in my life. It seemed as though in my mind that I could never measure up or be enough to fit in. I was told by a very strong lady that "If I put anything before a loving God it shall be removed." Keeping God first eliminated the pressure of what others think and say and it eliminates a lot of unnecessary anxiety. It's time to be set free from living your life trying pleasing people, who are also trying to do the same insane thing,

Recovery Insight: God first…No matter what!

Day 31
If you always do what you've always done, then you'll always get what you've always got.

Insanity is always looking for something different in the same actions. Wanting something different requires doing something differently. Complaining doesn't change anything but, doing something different does!

Recovery Insight: Change comes from within…No matter what!

Day 32
People don't plan to fail…they fail to plan.

Never does a person plan to fail, unless you are self-sabotaging. When we do not plan we fail we fail to get what we desire. Making daily plans creates a more successful and fulfilling day.

Recovery Insight: Planning is the key…No matter what!

Day 33
You must change people, places, and things. Basically, you must change everything.

When you are changing your life, you must also make changes in your life. Having the same people in your life stagnates your life. People are circles of influence. They influence your character and your dreams. Going the same places and doing the same things result in the same results

Recovery Insight: Change everything…No matter what!

Day 34
If you deny what's real and you hide life's pains, only a fantasy remains. #Dexter A.

If you do not deal with issues within your life eventually they will deal with you. Facing your problems instead of masking them or ignoring them helps you to heal from them and to control them. Otherwise the life you live will be forced and fake.

Recovery Insight: Free yourself of fantasies…No matter what!

Day 35
The results of active addiction is jails, institutions, and death.

Eventually, the addict in active addiction will encounter the fatal consequences of either psychological or physical incarceration, derailment or breakdowns. Your addiction is powerful, cunning and baffling taking you places in your life that you have never dreamed or dared to go.

Recovery Insight: The results of active addiction is painful…No matter what!

Day 36
A man is considered rich when he is satisfied with what he has. #Dexter A.

Contentment is not complacent but the catalyst of acceptance of God's plan for your life. Life is so much sweeter and serene when you can be grateful for what you have and not compare your life with others.

Recovery Insight: Loving my life…No matter what!

Day 37
You win or lose in life according to the choices that you make.

The choices that I make determine the path that I take in my life. The path I take determines the direction that I travel. The direction that I travel determines my destination. I can always change my direction if I change my path through my changed choices. I can win or I can lose…I choose.

Recovery Insight: I am responsible for my destination…No matter what!

Day 38
To surrender is to win

This is a major oxymoron in one's life. We are instructed by most of our encouragers in life to "never quit, never give up" This is one time in life we are encouraged to quit using, to give up the high cost of low living and quit hanging with these toxic people. In recovery, it is essential for one to surrender in order to win.

Recovery Insight: I can't do this anymore…No matter what!

Day 39
This is how we do it: Honesty, open-mindedness and willingness.

Self-honesty is the beginning of to a new way of life. Once I am able to confront myself I have the potential to conquer this disease of addiction. Once I realize and accept that I have a problem that I am powerless over, that makes my life unmanageable, then I am open-minded to suggestions which leads me to a turning point of willingness to surrender my will and my way in my life to a better new way of life.

Recovery Insight: This is HOW I DO IT…No matter what!

Day 40
Only when I learn to love myself am I able to free myself and live.

When I really love myself, I will not do anything to intentionally harm myself. I will make decisions that will benefit me in my life. I learn to make decisions that will benefit me and those that I love. I can love others not expecting them to do anything in return for me. Loving me liberates me from self-destruction and enables me to love others.

Recovery Insight: Love has everything to do with it…No matter what!

Day 41
*Life is too short to hold on too long,
to old shame and pain.*

Things that I am powerless over prevails me the opportunity to let free and full when I try to hold to them. Unmanageability causes stress to occur in one's life which causes sickness and loss of serenity. When I acknowledge and accept that I cannot change my past and I will not allow it to control me any longer that I find peace and liberation.

Day 42
Sometimes God will change your circle to save your life.
#Dr. Tammy

The people that we share most of our time with are our circles. These people tend to directly or indirectly affect our life decisions. When those in our circle are a hindrance to bring out our life given purposes. God will remove them from our lives to reposition our mind choices.

Recovery Insight: Changes change our life…No matter what!

Day 43
God is not punishing you but, preparing you for the purpose which he promised for your path in life. #Dr. Tammy

There are times in our life that we experience heartache, trials, and tribulations. Sometimes, we find ourselves all alone, locked up, fired, divorced, or even dealing with painful situations like death. No matter what we may encounter in our life I must accept it is all part of my assignment to fulfill my destiny in my life.

Recovery Insight: Pain prepares us for a purpose…No matter what!

Day 44
Don't make any major decisions alone during your first year of recovery. #Dr. Tammy

My decisions and best choices landed me in the situation I am in therefore I must accept that my decision-making ticker isn't ticking properly. Until I learn to make healthy choices I must surrender to the fact that I am not capable of making healthy and sound decisions. Therefore, I will accept suggestions from others with quality time in recovery.

Recovery Insight: My future depends on my help…No matter what!

Day 45
This too shall pass…Anonymous

Everything must change. Believe it or not you will not always feel the way you feel. The problem that you have right now will not last forever. Weeping may endure for a night, but joy comes in the morning (Psalm 30:5 KJV). Its good to know that trouble don't last always! Sometimes when we are going through trials and tribulations it feels as though it will last forever and that it will never end, but be assured that things will change. If you continue to do the right thing for the right reason, eventually things will turn in your favor. Whatever you are going through always remember that it will pass. The sun will come out tomorrow in your life if you weather the storm and never give up!

Recovery Insight: Never allow your problems to intimidate your faith …. No matter what!

Day 46
Nothing outside of me can help my insides.
#Dr. Tammy

Money, food, sex, drugs or career advancements cannot fix the void that lies within. Nothing externally can fix my unkind problem. Until I work on fixing the core of me everything else is really only a

Recovery Insight: It's in me…No matter what!

Day 47
Unhealthy relationships are like drugs. They control change and convolute my sanity. #Dr. Tammy

"You attract that which you are" so be honest about where you are in your recovery before you begin reaching based on your desires and wants as opposed to what is best for you.

Recovery Insight: Build healthy relationships…No matter what!

Day 48
Any addict CAN recover! #Marisa

If you can believe and you are willing to work it then it will work for you. Recovery is work but, it is worth it. When you get sick and tired of being sick and tired then you are a candidate for recovery.

**Recovery Insight: Recovery is a process but, it does happen…
No matter what!**

Day 49
When the pain of remaining the same becomes greater than the pain of changing, we will change.#Anonymous

If there is no pain then there is no motivation for change. The pain of not changing and staying the same endorses and encourages one to want to change. Fear and pain are powers greater than ourselves that propels change.

Recovery Insight: Pain ignites change…No matter what!

Day 50
Nothing happens until the pain of remaining the same outweighs the pain of change. #Anonymous

Day 51
Change happens when the pain of holding on becomes greater than the fear of letting go.
 # Anonymous

Pain must outweigh fear. When the pain is much greater than fear, I lose my fear due to desire to rid my pain. #Dr. Tammy

Recovery Insight: Pain stimulates change…No matter what!

Day 52

I've got to allow some pain to remain in, in order to have the motivation to change. #Dr. Tammy
Nothing changes if nothing changes if you always do what you've always done, you will always get what you always got.! #Anonymous

When there is no longer the memory of pain I will repeat the action again. I was often reminded as a child that if I played with fire I will eventually get burned. I must hold on to the memory of the pain associated with my using to remind me why I cannot take that first one.

Recovery Insight: I can't take the first one…No matter what!

Day 53
Pain will push you to be desperate, determined, and dedicated. #Dr. Tammy

Surrendering to the disease of addiction and recovery begins with desperation. That's the first step to recovery. Pain induces desperation. When I first enter recovery, there is a sense of desperation that is so prolific because of the pain from my using. The longer that I stay around in recovery. I then become determined to stay clean and later I find myself dedicated to the life of recovery.

Recovery Insight: There are 3 D's to Recovery…No matter what!

Day 54
To block someone from hitting their bottom is to block someone from recovering. # Dr. Tammy

Hitting your bottom is essential to developing a mindset of total surrender. When loved ones continue to block you from hitting that brick wall, they block you from feeling the pain and from recognizing the need and desperation for change. Until a person feels the pain they will struggle with the need for a change. Loving someone to death is doing everything you can to prevent them from dealing with the wreckage of their actions and facing the reality of their decisions. Until we are able to see and acknowledge the severity of the disease and the negative impact that it is having on our life we will continue down the same destructive path. Tough love is allowing us to feel the pain and make the decision to change.

**Recovery Insight: Hitting rock bottom helps us surrender …
No matter what!**

Day 55
No matter what you encounter in your journey of recovery remember to stay the course. # Dr. Tammy

It is so easily to get distracted with family issues, health issues, job issues, or relationship issues. It is important to not put anything before your recovery. If you put anything before your recovery you will lose it. Without recovery you will not be able to keep all things that you have acquired. Your recovery will help you to have balance in your life and eliminate the stress of unmanageability. Practicing the spiritual principles in the steps is the key to a happy, joyous, and free life. Meeting makers make it, Step workers can take it! It is important to make the meetings, 90 meetings in 90 days and work steps with your sponsor. Recovery is making changes in your life. Making changes happen in step work.

Recovery Insight: Keep your recovery first in your life…No matter what!

Day 56
God can and God will, if you just let him. # Dr. Tammy

God can heal restore, deliver and see free if you are willing to give yourself to him and leave it there. Every time we try to fix our life on our own we make a mess of things. When we make the decision to let go and let God have all of our problems that we cannot handle, we have made the best decision that we can make. Why try to handle something that is too big for you when you have a God that is bigger than your problem. When I learned to trust God with all my problems, it made my life a lot easier to handle and less stressful.

Recovery Insight: Letting go and Letting God works every time … No matter what!

Day 57

Getting high is not an option to my problems. I can never control my using, it always controls me. # Dr. Tammy

Ask yourself, Could I ever control my using?, How many times did I try to stop but I was not successful at staying stopped? Every time I tried to control my using, instead it controlled me. I could not control how much I used and usually could not control what I did when I used. Because, I accept I cannot control my using, I will accept that I cannot take that first one. Taking that first one is the most deadly move that I can make. My disease wants me dead and it will do whatever it can to manipulate my mind to pick up and use. I must be vigilant.

Recovery Insight: Using is not an option that I can control…No matter what!

Day 58
Self-centeredness is the core to the disease of addiction.
I want what I want no matter the consequences.
#Anonymous

When I am in my active addiction or in my disease mode I think with my desires not my logical thinking. I tend to take many risks and overlook the consequences. What I want becomes my primary focus and desire. I no longer think of those around me who will be affected by my decisions. Even after realizing the consequences I find myself so consumed with my wants that I ignore the negative consequences of my desires. Self-centeredness is the core to my disease of more. I must learn to focus on the consequences of my decisions and the impact that they will have on everyone around me including myself. Life is not just about me! Step work and service work teaches to me to more selfless, compassionate of others, and more loving of myself.

**Recovery Insight: My self-centeredness controls my choices…
No matter what!**

Day 59
*If you change your thoughts you can change the world.
The world won't change just your perception on the world.
#Wayne Saulters*

It's amazing that our perception shapes our decision making process. The way that I see things shape the way I think about things, and the way I process things. When I am in active addiction or my addiction mode, I find myself thinking irrationally and deconstructive. When I am applying spiritual principles to my life I find myself viewing life in a totally different manner. My lens of life change when I am working a program of recovery, that is why it is important that I do not make major decisions alone in my first year of recovery. The more I work my program of recovery the clearer I am able to see things in my life. Life does not change only the way I view it. If I want to see clearer I must change the way I think and that comes through reconstructive thinking.

Recovery Insight: Changing my lenses creates new sights and site…No matter what!

Day 60
You can't give what you don't have. You can't save anybody until you save yourself. #Anonymous

I cannot help others when I am trying to find my own way. I cannot save anyone when I am also lost. Until I have recovery and healing, I cannot give anyone advice, direction, suggestions or wisdom. Experience, strength, and wisdom come from living it and working a program of recovery. If I have not been through it and recovered from it I can't share about it! It's not enough to have just lived it, but having learned from it and being healed of it makes you capable of providing solutions to it!

Recovery Insight: Until I get it, I can't give it ... No matter what!

Day 61
Be careful not to get too hungry, angry, lonely or tired. H.A.L.T.!!! # Anonymous

Stop before you self-destruct. When we neglect ourselves of food, peace, company or rest. We set ourselves up for a fall or a possibly relapse. HALT is like a yellow flag that shouts WARNING!! When you find yourself feeling any of these feelings: hungry, angry, lonely, and tired, STOP and deal with these emotions. These are signs of relapse.

Recovery Insight: H.A.L.T. is a sign to stop and regroup … No matter what!

Day 62
I need to forgive myself before I can forgive others. #Dr. Tammy

The hardest person to forgive is you yourself. Once we can find the forgiveness in our hearts for ourselves we are able to be more compassionate to others and forgive them. We have the tendency to think of everyone else that we have harmed and forget about ourselves. If I cannot love myself, I cannot love you. It is the same with forgiveness, if I cannot forgive myself I cannot forgive you. Forgiveness is the key to self-psychological incarceration. If you want to be set free you must release yourself from the bondage of your past,

Recovery Insight: Forgiving myself comes first…No matter what!

Day 63
I've got to leave here to get there!
#Dr. Tammy

I must leave the place where I am if it is not happy, joyous, and free to get to my place of serenity. I must leave guilt, shame, worthlessness, and self-pride to get to a place of freedom---there. If I have the desire to go to a happy, joyous and free lifestyle I must be willing to leave the negative mindset that I am living in. Making the decision to be happy is an action move that requires me to mentally relocate and separate from my past and accept a new way of life.

Recovery Insight: I have to move from here to get there…No matter what!

Day 64
Enjoy the moment, it is a present. Learn from your actions, they are the past and allow your tomorrow to happen without future tripping. #Dr. Tammy

Learning to enjoy the moment that you are in without focusing on yesterday or but in tomorrow is where my relief comes from. When I can stay in the here and now and find appreciation and acceptance, then you can grow and glow.

Recovery Insight: Enjoy now…No matter what!

Day 65
Let your tape rock until the desire pops!
#Dr. Tammy

Run the tape of the pain that addiction caused in your life. Run the tape of the consequences of your active addiction until it rocks you. Until your crazy desperate. Run the tape until it pops. When the cravings come into my mind it is imperative that I think of all the negative consequences of my using before I act on my thoughts. I must remember that I am not responsible for my first thought, but I am responsible for my second thought. I must make my second thought be the thought of the pain that using caused. My tape is created by my first step in recovery. The list of my unmanageability that was caused by my addiction creates my reasons for not picking up. I must create my personal tape from my personal journey of destruction that my addiction has caused in my life. I must run this tape over and over again in my head until it pops and destroys the desire to use.

Recovery Insight: Run the tape and don't pick up ... No matter what!

Day 66
You can't let the chains of the past weigh you down...Let God break every chain and set you free.

You can't change the past so don't let your past hold you back or hold you down. Your past does not define your present or your future unless you allow it to hold you in captivity or bondage. As you work the steps and learn to let go and let God you will witness the chains of your past falling off of you. God is a chain breaker! If you want to be set free, let God remove your chains.

Recovery Insight: My past will not dictate my present, God can break my chains ...No matter what!

Day 67

Everything for my future depends on how I choose my next step…How I chose dictates my moves. #Dr. Tammy

My choices dictate my destiny. If I choose good healthy choices I will travel in healthy directions. Life is like a chess game, the choices I make dictate my moves which determines my position in life, win or lose! If I want better, I must choose better. If I want to change I must choose to change. If I don't like what is going on in my life I have the power to change it. All I have to do is ask God for the courage to change the things that I can. There are some things that I am powerless over such as people, places, and things, but I do have the power to make decisions to change me!

Recovery Insight: My choices dictate my direction … No matter what!

Day 68
Don't focus on what you can't be. Instead, work through to be what you want to be. #Dr. Tammy

If I focus on all the things that I can't be or can't do, then I will never do or become anything. Instead, it will profit me more to focus on what I can do. I have to learn to embrace what I have and who I am so that I can enhance my gifts and my greatness. What I can do today is change me for the better. I choose to move forward with what I have and not focus on what I do not have.

Recovery Insight: Focusing on what I can do gives me hope … No matter what!

Day 69
You have a birth date and a death date, make the "dash" matter. #Anonymous

There are two dates which we are not in control over, that is our birth date and our death date. However, we can control the days between those dates. The time we live and how we live are the most important. What will your "dash" say about you? It is important that the decisions I make in my life reflect the way that I want to be remembered.

Recovery Insight: The "dash" in my life matters…No matter what!

Day 70
It is better to understand than to be understood.
#Anonymous

It is not always so important that people understand us as it is that we understand people. Trying to get others to understand our point and our thoughts are not as important as it is for us to understand others. It reduces conflict and confusion. When I spend so much energy and time on attempting to convince someone of what I am thinking, doing, or have done as opposed to taking time to understand their point as well then I am not being open-minded. Actively listening to others and viewing life on life terms is part of living a healthy life of recovery. When I am practicing humility it allows me to remain teachable and meek.

**Recovery Insight: Understanding others is more important …
No matter what!**

Day 71
God has given me my own path to take. My own troubles to endure. My own good things to experience. I must own those things and not question the plan (bigger picture).
#Dr. Tammy

Sometimes it's difficult to accept the course of my life as the plan that God has for me. I must learn to accept life on its own terms and my life experiences as part of my self-development. Life happens and sometimes it deals us a hand of disappointments; however, learning to accept that there is purpose in my pain and my problems. I might not like what has happened but I must learn from why it happened. Everything that happens in our life is designed to provide us with preparation for our purpose.

Recovery Insight: My life issues are part of my life purpose … No matter what!

Day 72
Do not run on your emotions because you will eventually crash. #Dr. Tammy

If I allow my emotions to dictate my direction I am bound to experience an emotional roller coaster experience. I can also find myself running into destruction causing a crash in my life. Being emotionally driven can be quite exhaustive because I never know where I end up emotionally. I have a choice to either be driven my intellect or by my emotions. My intellect will drive me based on the positive or negative results; whereas, my emotion will drive me based on my feelings. Feelings change like channels on a TV when someone else is controlling the remote, it makes me act out of control.

Recovery Insight: Emotional roller coasters can cause severe highs and lows…No matter what!

Day 73
Be thankful for your trials and tribulations because they will help develop and mature you for your purpose. #Dr. Tammy

Every experience that I have endured have the potential to shape and form me for my purpose in life. If I struggle with my existence then it would help me to inventory the directions that I have traveled in my life. If I never had a problem I would never know that God solve them. My faith and gratitude is woven into the fabric of my life through my trials and tribulations.

Recovery Insight: My trials and tribulations can make me stronger and wiser…No matter what!

Day 74

The painful times I experienced in recovery were really God's way of teaching me the real opportunities he is blessing me with in recovery. #Dr. Tammy

When I feel as though I am being punished because of the struggles that I have endured when I have accepted and fulfilled all the suggestion given to me in the rooms of recovery is not a punishment but is part of the process of growing. For me to mature in life I must endure some trials and tribulations. These experiences make me stronger, wiser, and better. I mature through my struggles. Today I embrace my struggles as a part of my recovery and not as a punishment.

Recovery Insight: My blessings are in my burdens…No matter what!

Day 75

Denial is living a lie. Denial stops me from seeing the truth and stops me from recovering. #Dr. Tammy

When I refuse to face the truth, see the truth, or acknowledge the truth I am living a lie. When I am living a lie I am denying what is really happening. If I cannot recognize the unmanageability and the insanity that is existing in my life I will never change. Change happens when I make the decision that I am going to do something different than I was doing. Making a decision to do something different doesn't happen until I get sick and tired of being sick and tired of whatever is happening in my life.

Recovery Insight: Denial will prevent me from changing ... No matter what!

Day 76
Self-centeredness is the core to my disease of addiction .... I want what I want no matter the consequences.
#Anonymous

When I make decisions based on my selfish desires without taking into consideration the feelings and the impact that the decision will make on the lives of my loved ones that is self-centeredness. When I am making a decision to do something that I want knowing that it can possibly result in harm to myself or someone else that is a part of my disease. When I am having a disease with myself I must be vigilant over the decisions that I make because I am susceptible of making a decision that is self-centered and destructive.

Recovery Insight: Making decisions based on what I want and not what is best for me can be self-destructive ... No matter what!

Day 77
Horrible suffering can transform you into a humble servant. #Dr. Tammy

No matter what you go through in your life each experience is part of your assignment. The more painful your experiences the clearer your purpose. Everything that we experience in life is part of the preparation for our purpose. The farther your fall, the more humble and powerful your resurrection. Humility is built from some of the most horrific times within our lives. The greatest accomplishment that you can ever attain in life is that of a servant.

Recovery Insight: Learning to be a servant is the greatest accomplishment … No matter what!

Day 78
The proof is in the end result.
#Dexter Anderson

The race does not go to the swiftest but to those who endure to the end. You might start out in the back of the pack but it does not define your finish. Never allow your position to dictate your destiny. Continue to strive for the finish line no matter where you are positioned in the race. Don't give up before the race is over!!

Recovery Insight: It's not over til it's over ... No matter what!

Day 79
When the reward becomes greater than the pain. # Dr. Tammy

Change is difficult when you can't see the end result; however, it is important to focus on the reward of staying the course of recovery than focusing on the pain of change. My focus in life determines my direction in my life. If I focus on positive things I will get positive results.. I must view my recovery and living clean as my main focus and reward instead of all that I might have suffered or all that I have lost.

Recovery Insight:. My reward must mean more than my pain … No matter what!

Day 80
You will have many problems in life, but don't allow the problems to overcome your happiness. #Dr. Tammy

Life is full of swift transitions so don't get caught up in the changes and not appreciate the results. Just because we make decisions to make positive changes in our life will not prevent us from experiencing some heartaches and pains. It is important that we do not put all of our focus on our problems as opposed to the solutions to our problems. When we focus only on our problems we have the tendency to miss our blessings. Always remember that your good days will outweigh your bad days if you remain grateful and focused on the positives in your life.

Recovery Insight: Recovery brings more happiness than pain … No matter what!

Day 81
Just don't pick up that first one! #Anonymous

The first one is the most fatal one in our addiction. It's the first one that leads us to the second one and third one and so on. One is too many and a thousand is never enough. Learning to not to pick up that first one is key to staying clean. Not picking up that first one is where our power lies. Once we pick up that first one we lose our power. Realizing that there is no hope, no solution, no victory, no freedom, or answer is taking that first one is the key to surrender and the lock to never again.

Recovery Insight: I cannot pick up the first one … No matter what!

Day 82
Hope is a positive imagination. #Dr. Tammy

Hope is when you have the belief in something that you cannot see with your naked eye but you can see in your mind. HOPE is hanging on positive expectations. Being able to imagine the best in the midst of your dark situation in your life is the same as being able to have a positive imagination in a dark tunnel in your life. Having hope is having faith even though it looks hopeless.

Recovery Insight:. Hold on to your HOPE … No matter What!

Day 83
The disease is very cunning. It tells the mind what the body ought to do. #Dr. Tammy

The disease of addiction tells the mind that it can do things that it cannot do and it tells the mind that it cannot do things that it can. The disease of addiction is very cunning, manipulative, and baffling. The mind is designed to serve not to control the body. When in active addiction the addictive mind will control the body and everything the body does, you lose control of any responsible behaviors. I must always remain in control of my mind or my mind will control me.

Recovery Insight: The body is a slave to the mind when you are in active addiction … No matter what!

Day 84
Getting clean is easy but, staying clean is where it is. #Dr. Tammy

It is easier to get clean than it is to stay clean if you are not committed to your life of recovery. Many people feel as though they are in control of their disease because they have had a period of abstinence; however, they are not able to stay clean. The solution is learning to stick and stay. Staying clean is where the freedom to active addiction resides.

Recovery Insight: Staying clean is where your power to stay No is … No matter what!

Day 85
You can't conquer it until you confront it.
#Dr. Tammy

If you are not able to admit that you have a problem, you will never accept that the solution to the problem and surrender. It is impossible to conquer a problem that you have never acknowledged. I cannot beat something I have never accepted that I need to fight. Self-honesty is the foundation to my recovery. Until I am able to be honest with myself about myself I will never recognize nor accept my issues. If I am not able to recognize that I have issues I will never work on my issues, and if I never work on my issues I will never overcome my issues.

Recovery Insight: Until I can see my problem, I cannot confront my problem and if I do not confront my problem I will never conquer my problem … No matter what!

Day 86
Don't waste your time looking back at what you've lost. Move on, life is not meant to be traveled backwards. #
Anonymous

It will never benefit you mentally travel backwards in your life, eventually you will run into something and crash. Backing up is ok for a temporary move but driving forward is the direction which one must focus on driving their life. Focusing on what is in your past will hinder you from seeing the blessings of your present and having a glimpse at your future. Yesterday is your past, tomorrow is your future and today is your present. Are you future tripping (your tomorrow), stuck in the impossibility (your yesterday) or living in the here and now (your present).

Recovery Insight: Your today is a present, enjoy it … No matter what!

Day 87
We have problems, God has plans. # Anonymous

Anytime you feel as though your problems are overwhelming you and you cannot see your way through always remember to seek the one with the plan, God. God knows the plans that He has for you so seek him for the answers to your problems. If you had a problem with your car you would seek help from the manufacturer. Why not seek help for your problems from your creator, God.

Recovery Insight: God has the answers to all of my problems … No matter what!

Day 88
*Start where you are. Use what you have.
Do what you can. #Dr. Tammy*

The beginning to a great end starts with starting. Where you are is a good place to start. What you have is a good thing to start with. You are only expected to do what you can in life. Looking for more is a part of our disease because it gives you reasons to doubt, complain, and give up. Instead try being grateful for what you have trusting that God will bless you with more. You are right where you're supposed to be! Make the best of what you have and give your best for a great ending.

Recovery Insight: You already have enough to make a new start to make your life better ... No matter what!

Day 89
Breathe let go and remind yourself. This moment is the only one you know you have for sure. # Dr. Tammy

Stop stressing and future tripping over tomorrow. You are powerless over the future, but you have power over what you do today. Tomorrow is not promised and yesterday is gone, but today is what you have for certain. Take a deep breath and relax knowing that you only have to live One Day at a Time!

Recovery Insight: Today is the only day that you can make changes ... No matter what!

Day 90
These things you take for granted, someone else is praying for. #Dr. Tammy

Learn to be grateful for what you have. Someone is praying for what you already have. We have a disease of MORE! We have a tendency to always feel as though we need more and fail to take the time to be grateful for what we already have. Don't overlook your blessings looking for more stuff. Be vigilant over your recovery and your blessings remembering the time when you did not have what you have and you wanted what you got.

Recovery Insight: When I am grateful for what I have I will be blessed with more … No matter what!

There will be times during this journey of life on your road to recovery that you will began to doubt yourself and your disease will cause you to have Stinking Thinking (Negative Thoughts, Thoughts of Self Doubt and Thoughts of Hopelessness). Please use these Positive Affirmations to Stop those ANTs (Automatic Negative Thoughts). Look in the mirror and speak these messages into your thoughts.

Remember No matter what: You cannot successfully get High or Drunk period!

You are now a member of the NO MATTER WHAT CLUB!!

Positive Affirmations for Stinking Thinking

1. I am more than enough
2. I can recover
3. I don't have to live that way anymore
4. I can stay clean
5. I can recover
6. I do not have to be a slave to past anymore
7. I am the greatest mother
8. I am not a victim … I am an overcomer
9. I will be better than I was before
10. I am going to get pass my past
11. My past will not control me
12. I am responsible for my recovery
13. I will have my life back
14. I love myself
15. I am ok and you are ok
16. I deserve better
17. I will live my dreams
18. I will win
19. I will not be controlled by drugs or alcohol again
20. I will not be fooled by my disease again
21. I surrender to the program
22. I don't know everything but I'm willing to learn
23. It is what it is and I am a survivor
24. I cannot control others but I can control me
25. I will live and I will not die
26. My life is valuable
27. I am worth it
28. My past will not dictate my future
29. I have had enough I have changed
30. I will not go back

28. My past will not dictate my future
29. I have had enough I have changed
30. I will not go back
31. I will do whatever it takes to recover
32. I forgive myself
33. I forgive those who have hurt me
34. I will make it through this
35. I am changing all my people, places, and things from past.
36. I will not live in shame anymore
37. I am not the same person
38. I am a new person
39. I will not answer that phone call again
40. I will not accept that behavior anymore
41. I have purpose and meaning in my life
42. God loves me
43. God cares about me
44. I am never alone again
45. My past does not define my destiny
46. I am not that same person anymore
47. God will restore
48. I have the power to say NO
49. I will not take that first one no matter what
50. I am willing to take suggestions
51. I am a winner
52. I am greater because of my failures
53. I am beautiful
54. I am unique
55. I am special
56. I am not a disappointment
57. I got it this time
58. I can't change my past but I have changed
59. There is good in me
60. I will not give up no matter what